T0197320

THE CHRISTIAN PERSPECTIVE ON MENTAL HEALTH

DR. PAUL MCDOWELL

authorHOUSE®

AuthorHouse™
1663 Liberty Drive
Bloomington, IN 47403
www.authorhouse.com
Phone: 1 (800) 839-8640

Published by AuthorHouse   10/28/2016

ISBN: 978-1-5246-4766-7 (sc)
ISBN: 978-1-5246-4764-3 (hc)
ISBN: 978-1-5246-4765-0 (e)

Library of Congress Control Number: 2016918003

Print information available on the last page.

Scriptures taken from the King James Version of the Bible.

I. Introduction.. 1

II. Main Body 5
 - Research of the problem and the hypothesis 5
 - The Philosophical Look or Hypothesis 9
 - Challenges and Contrasts between the
   Christian perspective and the secular
   perspective of mental health. 11
 - Prior thoughts and results............................... 20
 - Methodology that was used to acquire
   information researched 23
 - Problems that occur because of the
   separation of the mentally ill from
   others in society 27
 - Some stereotypes and beliefs are
   learned or acquired from a person's
   environmental influences................................ 29
 - The Problem of the stigma that is
   attached to being called mentally ill 33
 - The effects of race on mental health................. 36
 - Training may or may not be a factor in
   the disconnection of church and those
   that are mentally ill 40

III. Results of Survey of the 100 people given surveys 45

- These are the questions and answers in graphs. 45

IV. Survey Results of the 25 that were interviewed 63

V. Conclusion..77
  - What can be done now to improve the
    relationship of the Christian church
    and those that are mentally ill? 77

VI. Definition of Terms...................................89

VII. References..93

VIII. Appendixes...97

Author

Dr. Paul McDowell is married to
Mrs. Ruthie G. McDowell

Bachelor of Theology
Masters of Christian Counseling
Doctor of Christian Counseling
Church Pastor
License Clinical Addiction Specialist-Associate
Retired Police Chief
Former U.S. Marine

FOREWORD

What I found out in dealing with mental issues, is a lot of family members are not aware of how serious mental illness is. They neglect to seek further help in how to deal with their family members. Some actually become afraid of their family members. The patient sometimes began to self-medicate and stop using their medication and become drug abusers. When the family member become afraid of the family member with mental illness they leave it up the professional to deal with it because they no longer want to. Eventually, they are place in nursing homes or other places. Reading this book would help in dealing with family members with many different types of mental illnesses. There are so many mental issues and this book will allow the Christian to pray specifically for their family member's mental illness and get a better understanding the mental illness that their family member is experiencing.

Linda Gerald, Psychiatric Attendant at a Local Hospital

INTRODUCTION

There are many challenges for the mentally ill that should be addressed, However only one focus will be dealt with in this book and that is obtaining a general look or perspective of the Christian society toward those with mental health issues. Here are some sources that contributes to the perspective of what is good sound mental health and what are some deficits that are classified by various mental health professionals.

"Answers given nowadays to the question 'What are the characteristics of a mentally healthy person?' are likely to refer to such signs as the capacity to cooperate with others and sustain a close, loving relationship, and the ability to make a sensitive, critical appraisal of oneself and the world about one and to cope with the everyday problems of living. At other times of places, different qualities would have been mentioned, according to the values prevailing in the culture. For the English middle class at the turn of the 19th century, mens sana in corpore sano – a sound mind in a sound body – would have included a disciplined intelligence, a well-stocked memory, qualities of leadership appropriate to the person's station, a respect for morality, and a sense of what life means. There was at that time an absolute refusal, as Clouston (1906) put it, to admit the possibility of a healthy mind in an unsound body, or at all events in an unsound brain. Nowadays we regard mental health as attainable by even the severely crippled. Brain injury may put limits on the degree to which social capacities can be developed, but it does not prevent their development altogether; the influence of the milieu may be as strong as that of the severity of the injury." (R. L. Gregory (Ed.), 2004 p.576)

"Mark Tausig - Sociologists who study mental disorder work from a number of assumptions that define and distinguish their approach from other ways of understanding mental disorder. First, sociologists may view mental disorder as a normal consequence of social life caused by structured inequality rather than as a form of individual dysfunction. Second, they may regard mental disorder as the outcome of social processes that include the labeling of deviant behavior and stigmatic societal reactions to those labels. Third, they may define the object of study as psychological distress rather than as specific psychiatric disorders. Fourth, they may view the mental health treatment system as an institution for the social control of deviant behavior. Finally, the sociological perspective is concerned with proprieties of groups and populations and it is less informative regarding individual and clinical concerns. Although not all sociologists employ all of these assumptions in their research and some of these assumptions have generated considerable debate, collectively they represent what is distinctive about the sociological study of mental disorders.

The psychiatric medical model accounts for mental disorders as a function of individual biological reactions to environmental (including social) hazard and / or individual biochemical or genetic dysfunction – the brain. Biological psychiatry now dominates the way psychiatrists explain the origins of mental disorder and the way disorder is treated. The social causation model by contrast accounts for psychological distress as a function of the effects of positions in social structures of inequality.

Sociologists argue that disorder or distress arises from a stress process in which eventual, chronic, and traumatic stressors represent risks to well-being. In turn, individuals can mobilize resources to offset the effects of stressors and, broadly speaking, the balance between risk and protective resources determines the psychological consequences of stressors." (Tausig, 2007 p.2951)

Mental illness is looked at different in many parts of the world and in many circumstances; even suicide is looked at different in many different cultures and different countries. The way people look at suicide in American versus other countries is different especially in war time situations. Suicide by the Japanese soldiers in recent wars were viewed the same way suicide was viewed by the samurai warriors many years ago, as honorable in a wartime situation and they called it hara-kiri. There are also the Islamic Middle Eastern people that are terrorist that commits suicide by blowing themselves up killing others around them primarily because of their beliefs in their god or to create terror. But in the United States to commit suicide in battle is considered cowardliness and or crazy. Nevertheless, United Sates Marines are trained to jump on bombs that are thrown in a crowded area of Marines that will die unless the bomb is smothered by someone to absorb the impact. So being normal can vary from country to country and in different branches of services in the same country. It just depends on who or what entity and how they see this as normal for their group.

Main Body

Research of the problem and the hypothesis

There was research of the problem to be investigated and the disconnection of the Christian community from the mentally ill or those with mental health disorders. All efforts were made to investigate just how bad the disconnection between Christians and the mentally ill really is. The disconnection and misunderstanding of the problem seems to be very serious and the survey process shows some of the problem with the variation of the answers to the questions that were presented to test the disconnection. There were some recommended referrals of the mentally ill the police for help. The police are knowledgeable of services that are available, but the police cannot be a cure-all type of agency for all situations.

There were of course some limitations to the researching of the problem. It was impossible to reach out to everyone one, however I was able to sample various populations and possibly improve the level of awareness and knowledge of the sampled population that have a basic knowledge of mental illness and or helping someone with mental illness. This inquiry and survey process has challenged a lot of people to think about their involvement in the life of individuals that are mentally deficient of operating in normal everyday activities and are in need of someone to take care of them or give guidance. This process of surveying has challenged some of those that were thinking of the mentally ill as people that need a helping hand from them or someone that is able to help. The People that were surveyed were from a variety of places such as North Carolina, South Carolina, Virginia, Georgia, and Florida and some people were originally from other countries such as the Bahamas, but now reside in the United States. Some of surveys were completed on a ship, thus it helped with the variation of locations that the people were from that completed the surveys.

Assumptions asked and answered – There were assumptions that some people will resist any attempt to create or express relationships with the mentally ill. **Just a few people responded with the answers indicating that the mentally ill need to care for themselves, or be taken care of by someone other than them (them, being the ones that completed the surveys). There was also an indication that the people that are trained in the specific areas of work with mentally ill are the ones that need to take care of the mentally ill.**

There were relevant concerns about the research project and question concerning the approach.

There were materials that were available to assist with obtaining the needed relevant information concerning the disconnection from those that have mental illness. **Even though there were materials available that dealt with the disconnection of society and the mentally ill however there were very little that have been found that talks about the disconnection of the church and the mentally ill. This was very interesting because it either tells me that very little thought occurs about this or there is very little concern about the disconnection between the mentally ill and the church or the religious society. So very little is available to deal with this problem and I have found very little to give direction to improving his existing problem.**

What new approaches and suggestions can be made relevant concerning mental health issues that Christians can incorporate in their everyday approach to improve their awareness and their involvement in the life of those that have mental illnesses? One start with dealing with this issue is below.

"Educational approaches to stigma to challenge inaccurate stereotypes about mental illness and replace these stereotypes with factual information. This can be accomplished by providing basic facts about mental illness to an audience, or by contrasting myths with facts about mental illness. The goal is not to make the audience experts on mental illness, but rather to provide simple facts that many of the myths about mental illness crumble (Watson & Corrigan, 2001)." (Corrigan, 2005 p. 284)

Surely there are many myth and misunderstandings about the mental illness of an individual. Some things that are believed or that are said by people are so far off track that it is hard at times to understand the reasoning behind what they believe. The beliefs of people are their reality and not necessarily the truth of the matter and not truly the reality of the matter but it is what they believe. All of these false thoughts and beliefs contribute to the disconnection between a large portion of society and the mentally ill.

The Philosophical Look or Hypothesis

There is a great disconnection between the Christian community and the mentally ill. The disconnection is shown in the way that the mentally ill is over looked or ignored. In some situations, some people believe the mentally ill have a type of disease that can be transmitted to them by simply being around the mentally ill person too often or being involved in the lives of the mentally ill person on a continual basis. Do people really believe that somehow they can become affected mentally by dealing with or living with people that have mental health issues? Some people feel that all mentally ill people are different and act so different that they don't want to get the mentally ill person started with their allusions and strange reactions because they are just crazy and there is nothing that can be done by Christians to help them but to pray for them. People do not want to deal with anything that is different from them or deal with something or someone that they do not understand. People do not want to deal with new challenges or things that are different and or things that they do not understand if for no other reason because of the fear of the unknown. The fear of the unknown keeps a lot of people from reacting positive or showing the caring side of them. The fear of the unknown is a type of barrier that causes a spirit of separation in many cases in which there would be relationships between them and the mentally ill person. Positive relationships that would be very encouraging and profitable to the point of bringing about enrichment in the life of all individuals involved will never have a chance to develop. If people could just get more involved with others it would create relationships that would become examples for others to follow that would improve communications and the life of many people that needs a relationship with someone.

There were various challenges and two of them are:

Variables – People in different parts of the world are different in the way they deal with problems and issues in general. What is normal in the United States is not necessarily accepted as normal in other countries and societies, and what is normal in other countries in many cases is not normal in the United States.

Measures of variables – The measurement of the various variables in mental health beliefs and acceptance are numerous and cannot be dealt with but there is a more focused attempt to cover a reasonable amount of information that will be clear as to the thoughts and approaches that need to occur to make a reasonable difference in the disconnection of Christians and the mentally ill. There is some significance of the Research because it shows some need for improvement in the relationship of Christians and the mentally ill.

Challenges and Contrasts between the Christian perspective and the secular perspective of mental health.

Secular Research

The secular approach to mental health is purely the scientific approach to behavior awareness and behavior change. The secular approach is systemic and direct as to the way to change the dysfunctional to functionality.

Christian and Secular points of interest -

"Despite this controversy, there are many signs that the role of religion in health care is increasing. For instance, the Diagnostic and Statistical Manual of Mental Disorders, Fourth Edition, recognizes religion and spirituality as relevant sources of either emotional distress or support (Kutz, 2002; Lukoff, Lu & Turner, 1992; Turner, Lukoff, Barnhouse, & Lu 1995). Also, the guidelines of the joint Commission on Accreditation of Healthcare Organizations require hospitals to meet the spiritual needs of patients (La Pierre, 2003; Spiritual Assessment, 2003). The Literature has reflected this trend as well. The frequency of studies on religion and spirituality and health has increased over the past decade (Levin et al., 1997). Stefanek and colleagues reported a 600 percent increase in spiritual and healthy publications and a 27 percent increase in religion and health publications form 1993 to 2002 (Stefanek, McDonald, & Hess, 2004)." (P. McNamara (Ed.), 2006 p. 37)

There seems to be very little increase in interacting on a joint basis for the Christian community and the mental health community. Very little information is or will be shared by each part of these two communities if for no other reason because of confidentiality concerns or the lack of trust in each other. I do not know if confidentiality is the problem or the excuse that is used to keep road blocks in place so there are no communications or shared information by the Christian community, and the mental health professionals. For whatever the reason this does not help the cause and the need for lives to be improved through collaboration.

There are always some things that need to be considered and also a need to look at its relevance.

The following are other questions that need to be addressed from literature that already exist.

"Use of Mental Health Services. It is important to understand how religious beliefs and practices influence the seeking of mental health care and the compliance with health treatments. Questions that need attention include:

- Do devout religious beliefs and practices increase or decrease the need for professional mental health services?

- Do religious beliefs and practices increase or decrease the likelihood of seeking such mental health services?

- Are there particular religious beliefs systems that are more or less likely to block the seeking of professional mental health care when necessary?

- Does devout religiousness increase or decrease the likelihood of compliance with psychiatric treatments either psychotherapy or biological treatments such as antidepressant medication or ECT?

Research in Special Populations. There is relatively little information on the religion – mental health relationship for certain mental conditions and subgroups in the population. Given this lack of information studies of religions impact are especially important in these groups.

Persons with Severe and Persistent Mental Illness

- What are the effects of religious beliefs and practices on the etiology and the course of severe mental illnesses such as schizophrenia, severe personality disorder, and current depression or bipolar disorder?

- How are the religious beliefs and practices of persons with severe and persistent mental illnesses or psychosis different from those of persons without these disorders or with milder forms of them?

- What are the biological and psychodynamic causes of religious delusions and how do they influence the course of illness?

- How do religious conversion experiences (sudden vs. gradual, in one religious group vs. another) influence mental health, and are there any biological explanations for this?

- How can religious communities' best support those with severe mental illness? What are the limitations of support?" (Koenig, 2005 p. 260, 261)

Here are some answers to the questions from before:

Do devout religious beliefs and practices increase or decrease the need for professional mental health services?

It somewhat decreases the need because of the belief of some people is that all strange behavior is because of demons. I believe what is in bible concerning the

existence of demons but in some situations mental illness is the cause of the behaviors that is exhibited.

Do religious beliefs and practices increase or decrease the likelihood of seeking such mental health services?

Religious beliefs in some situations decrease the likelihood of individuals seeking help from secular resources such as mental health and psychiatric professionals. This can go both ways because of the total belief that the problem can only be spiritual (demonic) or the total belief that the problem can only be from mental dysfunction or deficiency.

Are there particular religious beliefs systems that are more or less likely to block the seeking of professional mental health care when necessary?

I think it just depends on the individual person that is religious and/or mentally ill even though there are articles that discourage seeking help for mental health.

Does devout religiousness increase or decrease the likelihood of compliance with psychiatric treatments either psychotherapy or biological treatments such as antidepressant medication or ECT?

Yes, it will decrease the likelihood of compliance of psychiatric, psychotherapy, and biological treatments. From talking with people that are religious and in need of taking medicines for their disorder they usually say that they are waiting on their healing from the Lord. I believe God can heal anything but I also believe that God has given the doctors the ability to help bring comfort to those that have an illness.

The Electroconvulsive therapy (ECT) is a technique, complete under general anesthesia, in which small electric currents are passed through the brain, this intentionally triggers a brief seizure. The ECT appears to cause changes in brain chemistry that can quickly reverse symptoms of certain mental illnesses. It often works when other treatments are ineffective. Much of the stigma attached to ECT is based on early treatments in which high doses of electricity were administered without anesthesia, leading to memory loss, fractured bones and other serious side effects. But as for Electroconvulsive Therapy (ECT) I do not believe that this type of therapy is needed for anyone and believe that Christians would not accept this type of therapy for them or for their loved ones.

What are the effects of religious beliefs and practices on the etiology and the course of severe mental illnesses such as schizophrenia, severe personality disorder, and current depression or bipolar disorder?

Today it seems that more people are more accepting of the idea of major mental disorders than just a few years ago. I'm sure religious beliefs contribute to the beliefs and thinking of individuals with problems but not sure of the effects of the research of the origin of the mental health problem.

How are the religious beliefs and practices of persons with severe and persistent mental illnesses or psychosis different from those of persons without these disorders or with milder forms of them?

I think the more severe the mental illness the more probability that there could be a greater disconnect from beliefs of God and the acceptance of themselves as being a spiritual being.

What are the biological and psychodynamic causes of religious delusions and how do they influence the course of illness?

Some scientist believe that religion plays a big part on the mental health of the person negatively or that these individuals have delusions because of their religion, but I believe that religion helps the people to be more

grounded and have hope that their situation will get better and that they can changed.

How do religious conversion experiences (sudden vs. gradual, in one religious group vs. another) influence mental health, and are there any biological explanations for this?

I do not believe religious conversions influence mental health as for as adding to or causing mental illness. I believe that in some situations the problem that a person is experiencing is a demonic problem rather than having mental problems. As for as one religious group having mental illness more than another religious group there is no more difference than one segment of society in general having mental illness more than another segment, this just is not true, mental illness in not more prevalent in one versus another.

How can religious communities' best support those with severe mental illness? What are the limitations of support?

This can be done by working together with secular counseling organizations in the area of counseling those with the problem. Also religious Counselors can provide Christian counseling along with the various other forms of assistance for the mentally ill like support groups and other civic groups that perform

a service who are familiar with working through the mental health issues that exist. The biggest limitation that I see is some people that would get involved or help others does not have sufficient training or knowledge of the mental illnesses that exist and does not have the knowledge of what can be done to help those with mental illness.

Prior thoughts and results

Preliminary Statistical Analyses – Research and data that was collected before the survey is completed and applied to the disconnection was gained through a verbal process of communicating with various individuals from various walks of life over a period of years. These are some statements that people have made concerning people with mental illness that I have heard them say while I was working as a law enforcement officer.

Some people have made statements such as "I don't like to deal with people that are crazy (mentally ill) I don't even want to be around them". "There should be something that can be done about those people being on the streets and being able to walk up to you at any time." Some people have suggested that "the government needs to build more mental institutions and put crazy people in them". People have said they "do not want to deal with mentally off or crazy people every day on the streets and there should be something that someone can do about them being loose". People have said "they feel funny being around crazy people because it makes them feel like they are going crazy watching and hearing them talk crazy all the time". Numerous times I have heard people say "they are afraid to be around people that are crazy because they are afraid they will go crazy too".

It is good that not everyone thinks the same way about people that have mental illness but there are quite a few people that feel mentally ill people need to be locked up or need to be away from everyone else that are so called normal. There are even some situations in the bible where people were dismissed or rejected because they were living with mental problems. Just look at the problem that Jesus had to deal with concerning the man that had the legion of demons in him. The man was depressed and oppressed by his condition and lack of help to get rid of the demons that just had to have affected his mental state of being. The people in the area were more interested in him being locked up because he had been chained many times and he had broken the chains or fetters that were put on him to control him. He was also isolated from society and had to live in graveyards. The man was demon possessed and possibly deeply depressed from being oppressed by the demons. There was no hope for him but the Lord showed up on his behalf. The people were not happy about the man being healed of his condition. First of all, the demons were now gone from the man and the depression that the man had was now gone and the man was sitting calmly, he was talking, clothed in his right mind and now wearing appropriate clothing. The people once they found out what had happened did not want Jesus to be around them or in the area. They were upset because of the change in another person's life and of course their swine.

In general people want some type of change in the way that the mentally ill people act, but most do not want to be the one that help or facilitates the change. In some instances, people do not care if the person changes as long as the person does not bother or be around them. Christians need to have a little more love and try to help in any way that they can to assist the mentally ill with getting the help that they need.

Methodology that was used to acquire information researched

Research Approach

The research information is obtained from various information sources such as individual authored books, reference books that have being published by entities, and research groups. Research was from the internet and also psychological and counseling manuals. This research was not all encompassing but it was a type of comprehensive research.

Surveyed Population

The research population has been from age 18 to 90 years of old, but not limited to those ages if information could be obtained from some other age groups that were not recorded and did contribute much.

Surveyed Sample

The sampling reached out to primarily the Christian community, various groups, and different races of people. This was done to seek out the thoughts and understanding of those communities and try to challenge them to at least think a little more about the mentally ill.

100 surveys were distributed to individuals to feel out and an additional 25 people were interviewed and those surveys were completed by the person presenting the survey. This process presented opportunity that

challenged individuals to think about their involvement or their lack of involvement in the life of individuals with mental illness or even those with a developmental disability (M.R.).

The following are some procedures of when, where, and how the data was collected. There was a comprehensive survey developed and sent out to a wide range of people with hopes to get as many as possible back that have been filled out. Some surveys were completed by the developer interviewing the individual surveyed in person. Of course there were some critical concerns such as Reality vs. Perception, is there a way to challenge or change the person's perception of the mentally ill thereby changing the reality that they previously held in belief? The only way to change perception is to change the way someone looks at a situation and what they perceive is going on in the situation that they are looking at and experiencing. It's hard not to believe what you perceive to see or what you believe or perceive that you know.

There was question of communication and response to the survey. The questions such as will people respond to or fill out the surveys that were distributed? Will people that respond to the surveys answer the surveys with honest answers? Yes, there was great response to the surveys and the response was more positive than expected. I believe that most people shared their honest beliefs. But some had a tendency to try to answer the survey the way that they thought it was supposed or expected it be answered. I say this because in this survey process some people would say they were not sure how to answer the survey and then they would ask what is the answer to a question on the survey, they wanted to answer in way that was needed or that was expected.

There were questions of values. How did the surveys create importance and value for people to respond?

The survey gave individuals the opportunity to think through and give their opinion on something they said they really had not thought about before, therefore, they were given an opportunity to challenge the formal thoughts and or actions towards people with mental illness.

There was a question of unspoken assumptions(?). What was assumed by people because of the request to complete a survey about mental illness? Some people thought their information would not be used and some felt their information was not important so they asked me to just fill out the survey for them and that was only done with them answering the questions that were read to them. Some people responded to the survey by giving their opinion and giving me directions as to how to handle people that are mentally ill. Some statements were made such as "mentally ill are people too and you need to treat them like you would treat anyone else by showing them love, patience and respect." I feel that some people did gain new and open opinions of mental illness and they asked what would be somethings that they could do to improve their awareness of how to deal with people that have mental illness. There was no backlash but some improved attitudes towards helping people that are mentally ill.

Problems that occur because of the separation of the mentally ill from others in society

One of the problems that mentally ill people have is the lack of positive people that will lead them into a positive direction. Therefore, they are vulnerable to people that will do them harm or lead them into the wrong direction. There are also wrong groups or sects of people that mentally ill people are drawn to or get involved with because of their condition and the lack of positive people, information and resources available for them.

> "Harmful groups - The beneficial aspects of belonging to a group, be it religious or otherwise, are well-recognized in psychological and sociological literature. It is a matter of moral, ethical, religious, political and sometimes clinical opinion whether the influences of being part of a particular group have, or have not, been good for the individual and, hence, society. Definitions of groups that may be harmful derive from different epistemologies and can be ambiguous, pejorative and controversial (Barrett, 2001; Langone, 2007). Attempts at defining and understanding lead to polarization of views (Lalich, 2004). Although there are a good number of attempts at defining harmful spiritual groups, the following categories, from the cultic studies field will be considered:

- cults
- sects
- new religious movements
- charismatic groups" (Cook, 2009, p. 256, 257)

Separation by anyone from society causes or makes opportunity for an encounter with the wrong people when the person is in need of seeking help. For at some point in all of our lives we all need some type of help or assistance. My mother use to say treat everyone right because you never know who you will need help from before you leave this earth. She was talking about the possibility of one's health failing them one day and being in need of someone to help them and it might be the very one that has been mistreated by you and you end up needing help from them. This analogy works in everything and in every way that you may need some help by someone before you leave this world. I just feel that we are our brother's keeper and we will need to step up and assist people that are in need, that are lacking of care, and that need someone to see after them. The Lord tells us by way of the apostle Paul to bare one another's burdens or the strong should bare the infirmities of the weak. My interpretation of this is that we should take care of one another and take care of those who cannot care for themselves. Pray for one another and seek the Lord on behalf of ourselves and other people. I feel that the Lord is the only one that can give guidance to us for ourselves and /or guidance for someone else.

Some stereotypes and beliefs are learned or acquired from a person's environmental influences

One of the reasons there is a separation by some African Americans from the accepted societal standards of becoming well is because of the undergirded prejudices that seem to exist in established entities and programs that are set up to help individuals, however there has been a history of not being purely and forthrightly focus on the assisting of individuals of color that need true help to bring them from a state of pain to a state of healing and wellness. There are many authors that deal with prejudices and the origins of some of them. Here is one that deals with the origin of some prejudices from its beginning until it becomes part of a child's existence and belief unto their adulthood.

"Where do our stereotypes and prejudices come from? They are, of course, developed as all cognitive representations are developed, and we have a good idea of the cognitive process involved in this regard (Bigler, 1995; Bigler & Liben, 1992). Children have an active and seemingly innate interest in learning about social categories and stereotypes, and in understanding how to fit into this categorization system (Ruble & Martin, 1998; Stangor & Ruble, 1989). As a result, children learn stereotypes very early and become confident in them, such that they are initially highly resistant to change. Children soften their beliefs and become more flexible after age 10 or so (Bigler & Liben, 1992; Signorella, Bigler, & Liben, 1993). But what about the content? Most likely this knowledge comes from our parents, from our peers and from the media. Again, we have not been particularly interested in the issues of content, and the evidence about its development remains ambiguous. Frances Aboud, the world's expert on stereotype development, argues that there is virtually no relationship between racial attitudes of children and parents Aboud, 1988; Aboud & Amato, 2001). Other data suggest at least some correlation (Stangor & Leary, 2006)."

"Stereotypes matter because they are part and parcel of our everyday life, they influence our judgments and behavior toward individuals, often entirely out of our awareness (Bargh, Chen, & Burrows, 1996; Dijksterhuis, Aarts, Bargh, & Knippenberg, 2000; Wheeler & Petty, 2001). They become part of our everyday language (Maass & Arcuri, 1996; Maass, Salvi, Arcuri & Semin, 1989). These behaviors create self-fulfilling prophecies that bring out the stereotypes in their targets (Chen & Bargh, 1999; Word, Zanna, & Cooper, 1974). They are the cognitive "monsters" that poison many of our social interactions (Bargh, 1999)." "We tend to use our categories more when we are fatigued, distracted, or ego-depleted (Bodenhausen & Macrae, 1998; Govorum & Payne, 2006; Kruglanski & Freund, 1983), when the going gets tough (Stangor & Duan, 1991), or when we are little motivated to do more (Fiske & Neuberg, 1990; Neuberg & Fiske, 1987)." (T. D. Nelson (Ed.), 2009 p. 9)

This type of thinking puts individuals in categories prematurely and causes individuals to withdraw from any opportunity of help and opportunity for them to become a valuable part of society and life. Also stereotyping is not just done with race but it occurs with those that have mental health problems and / or homelessness and without the ability to take care of their selves. The stigma that occurs by the very mentioning of being mentally ill causing individuals to try to hide their condition and /or themselves from society and the demeaning statements and talking down to those whom are mentally ill individuals in which makes others feel they are better off according to societal standards. There should be a reaching out to the mentally ill by all including the Christian church of today that seems to preach prosperity but does very little to reach out to individuals that are in despair and downtrodden. The downtrodden, demoralized, and mentally disconnected individuals that are disenfranchised by some of the societal accepted ways of operating in which society calls normal living are somewhat on their own with the attempted recovery. The mentally ill live and operate in a world that will not accept them as being unique, being positive and able to contribute to society in any positive way. I know a lot of times we do not look at the way the mentally ill are treated as a type of prejudice reaction to people that are put in a group and classified as being crazy but it happens. So, what can be done to improve the way we look at others? Our greatest challenge is to change the thinking and reacting of individuals whom have all of their life categorized people to help them understand those that are different or deal with them or not deal with them that are different. It can be surprising a lot of times when we get to know a person that is different than the way we had thought them to be or what we noticed or glanced about them on the surface. Getting to know individuals occurs gradually in various settings or rather in settings that occur over time. In a lengthy period of time you can learn a lot about the person and also learn a lot about yourself. I think some of the reasons that people do not want to be around people that have mental illness is the fear of seeing in the mentally ill person some of the same traits or problems that they have on a smaller scale or even at the same level but it is controlled or the condition is hidden. Possibly we disassociate ourselves because of the fear of being classified as crazy, the fear of being stigmatized or the fear of being talked about. Everyone wants to be classified as normal, that's if there is to be any classifying at all.

The Problem of the stigma that is attached to being called mentally ill

No one wants to be called mentally ill or crazy because the word crazy is the word that most people use to categorize people that act or carry themselves differently from others. Being called crazy is ok when playing a sport and you are overly aggressive on a play but to be called crazy when you are not able to function like everyone else that are considered normal is what no one wants. No one wants to be singled out or picked on because of their shortcoming in an area of mental functioning especially when it seems like so many others are doing well. In a lot of African American communities, the family members that have problems of mental illness are looked at as being a family member that has a condition that no one can do anything about so just ignore it or put the person in the back room of the house, or in a mental institution. No one wants that type of treatment and no one wants that type of stigma attached to them. There are truly differences in treatments for individuals of various races with mental illnesses, but the stigma is still attached to them.

"The claim that minority – White American "underlying (mental) health conditions" differences – differences in treatment need – can legitimate minority – White American differences in treatment use has been met with little objection.

More controversial is AHRQ's proposal that minority – White American differences in treatment preference can legitimize treatment differences. In fact, treatment preferences can be socially conditioned, sometimes by circumstances we as a society should not accept. Like others but perhaps more so, African Americans sometimes reject mental health treatment because of the considerable stigma associated with mental illness (Alvidrez, Snowden, & Patel, 2010; Anglin, Link. & Phelan, 2006). In an interview, former Surgeon General David Satcher underscored stigma's entrenchment and power to thwart treatment seeking and recovery (American Psychological Association, 2009). Rather than acquiesce stigma-based treatment African American populations like those showing promise in preliminary research (Alvidrez, Snowden, Rao, & Bocellari, 2009)." (Snowden, October 2012 p.526) (H. P. Lefley & P. B. Pedersen (Eds.), 1986 p.131, 132)

The stigma of mental illness or the problem of not being treated the same whichever way you put it is one of the main problems in the treatment of African Americans for mental illness. The stigma along is enough to create a divide by African Americans from societal established standards of the process for recovery. When there is a difference in the treatments of African Americans by the status quo then there is of course more of a separation by African Americans from their needed treatment. The church itself creates a division by those in some churches saying that there is something wrong with you if you look for help in the secular community versus the Christian community alone. With some teachings on religious separation from any societal help there is also the same stigma added on to anyone that seeks assistance from the scientific community. The sigma increases from all angles of the community or society as a whole. The scientific community looks at mental illness as a money making profession in which at times there is no true care and recovery that is administered to improve the life of the mentally ill person. This is a problem that needs to be worked on to improve the quality of life for those who are hurting on the inside and at times take their own life and the life of others.

The effects of race on mental health

I cannot speak for those that are mentally ill, they are the only ones that can speak for themselves but this is an attempt to share what I have experienced from watching the despair and being lost in society that seems to exist because the lack of true help by the communities that the mentally ill are living in. The closing down of so many mental institutions does not help. The government has added themselves to those that show less and less care for those that are mentally ill. Then of course there is the lack of involvement by the Christian community in the life of the mentally ill person. The mentally ill seemingly are placed in a group or segment of their own by most people that misunderstand those that are experiencing a deficiency in their thought processes and maladaptive in ability to perform or take care of themselves in a normal way according to societal standards. Everyone wants to belong to something or have a connection to something that is positive and that makes them feel good about themselves. The race of a person can affect whether the person gets true treatment for his or her mental illness. Thus race, nationality, culture or even ethnicity is important to most everyone.

"Ethnicity, race, and nationality are often used interchangeably in our society. It is common to hear someone describing an individual's behavior, values, or beliefs by saying "he is African or she is Asia." These descriptions may be factual since the individual identifies with a country within those continents. However, after close interactions with the person you may find that they prefer a more specific description, such as Indian or Ghanaian. Furthermore, it may be even more important to them to identify with a specific ethnic or tribal group (e.g., Gujarati for the Indian, Ashanti for the Ghanaian, and Dina (Navajo) for a First Nations person. Interestingly these generalized descriptions are commonly made by people in the western world, but it is very rare to hear westerners describe themselves as Europeans or North Americans. Regardless of our assumptions, it is imperative to inquire about how an individual or a group views themselves."

"When cross-cultural interactions are not approached appropriately, clients are more likely to be misdiagnosed, receive inappropriate treatment, give up on treatment, and receive fewer benefits than their European American counterparts (Kurasaki, Sue, Chun, & Gee, 2000; Sue, Zane, & Young, 1994). Ethnic, cultural and other minority groups may view mental health services and institutions as inaccessible, unaffordable, culturally insensitive or otherwise inappropriate. Many have had personal negative experiences, such as experiences of racism or discrimination in similar institutions (e. g., health or educational). While others are weary based on collective histories and shared memories of oppression, genocide, enslavement, servitude, segregation, forced sterilization and unethical research practices. It is not surprising that many ethnic minorities have developed a certain level of mistrust for social service institutions. While this is often called a functional or healthy paranoia, this cultural mistrust also impacts help-seeking behavior." (S. Eshun & R. A. R. Gurung (Eds.), 2009 p.7, 116)

I feel the problem of being misdiagnosed occurs more often than most people think. The mentally ill that are minorities probably deals with misdiagnoses of their condition a lot more than the European Americans. This will cause minorities that have mental illnesses who hear of or have misdiagnosis to avoid the clinical assessment process and avoid any type of treatment that they may possibly need. Of Course, if there is even a small sign of racism minorities have in the past and will even now withdraw themselves from those that are showing any type of racist actions or any racial biases towards them. No matter what it is called functional or healthy paranoia the withdrawal will occur by the minority that needs the assistance. If someone thinks someone does not like them they will not trust the individuals with anything that is personal or life threatening because preservation or protecting oneself is the first value of anyone's life. How can this difference in assessment and treatment become better for the minority population? I don't know how to change those that are racist but those that work in mental health on the secular side of society need to work more with the Christian society and vise versus to create a trust that will bring about wholeness and recovery to those that are mentally ill of all races. The Christian part of society owes the Lord true representation to those that are in need of help and representation to make sure their rights are taken care of and that help and recovery occurs. The Lord has shown us grace in our everyday living and inaptness to glorify him with righteous living by accepting our request for forgiveness and recovery from our evil ways. Since the Lord has shown us mercy and grace even though we are not perfect like him, we must realize we must show mercy for those whom cannot help themselves. For by the very grace of God have we been received by him and have opportunity for a different life and even eternal life. We need to show mercy and show love to those that at different because of their mental condition.

Training may or may not be a factor in the disconnection of church and those that are mentally ill

The lack of training can always cause problems or give occasion for neglect of those that are hurt or that have no one to give them help or the right instruction for their need. As far as I am concerned there seems to be a great need for training of ministers in the area of mental health and counseling of people so that the assistance that they need can be given to them.

"Training in counseling, however, is often minimal, even among those who have years of postgraduate education, whether African American or Caucasian. The level of training that clergy receive is usually quite different from that actually needed to diagnose and / or manage individuals with short-term anxiety or depression, provide counseling for those with chronic mental illness, or deliver case-worker services for the chronically mentally ill. However, this is the level and type of mental health services that black clergy often must provide. Theological background and educational training also influence the likelihood of referral of church members to mental health professionals for further treatment. Ministers with more liberal theologies and more education are more likely to do so than those with conservative theologies and less education.

Interestingly, African American clergy are considerably more likely than white ministers to make referrals to community mental health centers. Taylor and colleagues discuss the role African American ministers in developing church-based programs with linkages to formal service agencies. The black church has long been a leader in providing a wide range of outreach programs, some of which involve addressing the mental health needs of black person without access to mainstream professional services.

Given the right economy and the reduction of community mental health services by states, which disproportionately affects African Americans, the role of the black church becomes even more important in terms of providing church-based services. There continues to be a strong ethos of community service in African American congregations that provides the motivation to meet the emotional and practical needs of those with mental illness, and their participation in the community programs is greater than that by white congregations – especially in those programs that address the needs of the poor. The church often functions as a mediator between African Americans and community service organizations, including community mental health centers and departments of social services. A study by Billingsley and Caldwell found that 50% of African American churches indicated that they collaborated with local mental health service agencies to provide community outreach programs. Twenty-eight percent of the support provided by African American churches was emotional in nature and focused on counseling and support groups." (Koenig, 2005 p.178, 179)

Even if the African American minister has to provide counseling to the mentally ill person there are very few African American ministers that are trained in the area of counseling and even less trained in the area of clinical / mental health counseling or Christian counseling. Even if the minister does not know the process of counseling he or she can recommend or refer the person to a provider or crisis management team in the area if the need is there and if the minister is aware of it. Lots of times the mentally ill person is in need of being referred but is not referred to anyone that can help them with their need because there is no one available that knows where to refer them to. There is a great need for more training and cross training for mental health professionals and ministers. I feel that the needed quality of counseling and care needs to increase for the parishioners that are in need of the mental health services. There is a need for improvement in the quality of life for the people in the community and in the church that needs mental health assistance. Until ministers show a desire to get more training and cross training in this area people will continue to suffer with no opportunity of getting help.

Results of Survey of the 100 people given surveys

These are the questions and answers in graphs

94 surveys were completed and turned back in from the 100 that they were given out = 94%.

Age of Person completing survey 21 – 85
Male 39   Female 55
Christian 76   Non-Christian 7   Deferred not to answer on religion 11

1. Can you become mentally ill because you spend long periods of time with someone that has a mental illness?

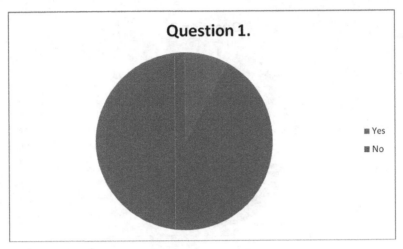

7 Yes 81 No

Answer:

There were a few that either knew about becoming depressed from being overwhelmed from being around someone that have a mental illness and they are continually saying the same things day in and day out. But there was not an overwhelming fear of being around someone that is mentally ill for long periods of time according to the answers.

2. Who should deal with the people that are on the streets and in the community that have mental illness?

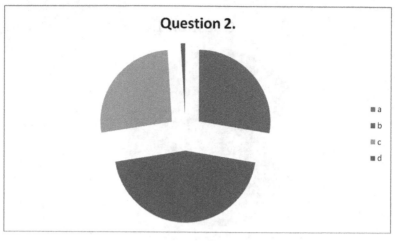

a. the police   b. providers only   c. you   d. They should be by themselves

27 a   44 b   26 c   1d

Answer:

Most people answered on this question provider's only, but some checked off the police also. Some people checked off two or three of them. One person did not think that the mentally ill person should get help from anyone one, just let him along.

3. Do you have an obligation to help the mentally ill?

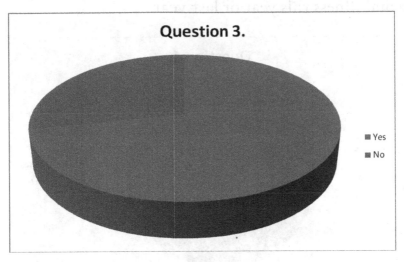

Question 3.

- ■ Yes
- ■ No

73 Yes 21 No

Answer:

Over the majority of people said they should have an obligation to help the mentally ill in some way but could not or would not say how they would help.

4. Have you assisted in any positive way someone that has mental illness this year or last year?

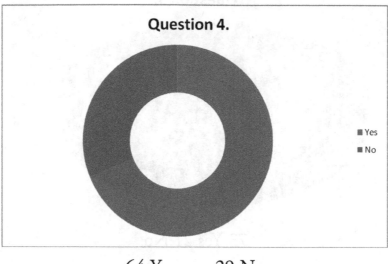

64 Yes   29 No

Answer:

A lot of people said they have done something to help a mentally ill person within the last year. Some could describe how they helped someone and some only said that they are sure they helped someone that was mentally ill.

5. Have you lived with someone that has a mental illness? If yes how long?

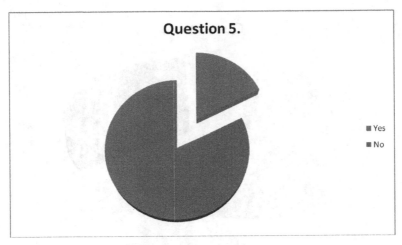

15 Yes   69 No
How Long: 10months to 20 years

Answer:

There should have been a larger yes response to this question than the response that was received. The reasons could have been that they did not want to disclose the information of a loved one having a mental illness, or the lack of ability to recognize the signs of mental illness.

6. What can you do to help someone get assistance with their condition of mental illness?

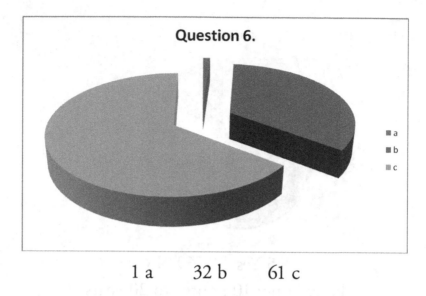

Question 6.

1 a   32 b   61 c

a. let them along   b. call the
police   c. get to know them

Answer:

The majority here of course said get to know them (mentally ill people) but some said call the police and of course one said let them along. We realize that people will give their best answer on a survey and a lot of times they will give the answer that they think is wanted instead of their true opinion.

7. Should the Christian church do something to help people with mental illness?

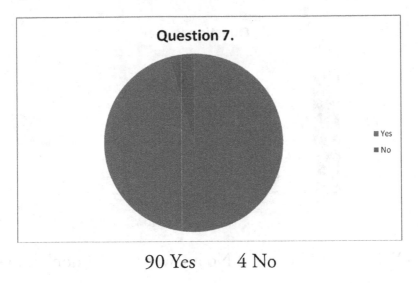

90 Yes   4 No

Answer:

The overwhelming answer was yes but very little comments on how the church should be involved or what the church should do to help others than to pray for them that have mental illnesses.

8. Do some individuals inherit mental illnesses from their parents or other ancestors in their family?

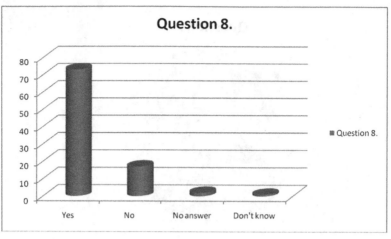

73 Yes   17 No   2 No answer   1 I don't know

Answer:

There were some concerns about the environment that people live in affecting their mental health and some behaviors that have actually come from being around those with mental illness type behaviors.

9. Is mental illness and mental retardation the same thing?

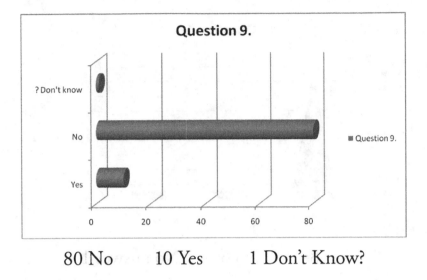

80 No   10 Yes   1 Don't Know?

Answer:

Most of the responses to the question were correct by answering no, but one surveyed did not know and did not want to guess the answer. Ten said yes mental illness and mental retardation is the same showing that some people are mistaken.

10. Can God cure a person from mental illness?

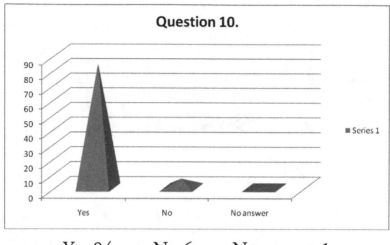

Yes 84   No 6   No answer 1

Answer:

The belief that God can cure someone of mental illness was an 89% response to the question out of 94 people that completed the surveys and majority believes God can cure mental illness.

Final Question of Survey of 100 surveyed:

What other comments do you have about people with mental illness?

These are the various comments that people made concerning people with mental illness:

Helping people with mental illness requires helping those that their life must have boundaries, stability, order and importantly God. They should be encouraged to go to the proper agencies.

Some said you can possibly become mentally ill by being around a person that is mentally ill for long periods of time.

Another said maybe someone can become mentally ill by being around someone for long periods of time that has mental illness but was not sure.

People with mental illness are no different than people with a physical illness, although society has differentiated the two in the way people with mental illness are cared for and viewed by society.

I think we should treat them with respect. Also help them with their issues that they are dealing with. Certainly have (prayer) with them often as possible.

They are human beings and I feel that they should be treated with the utmost respect, love and dignity. They need our prayers and our help.

Many times they are undiagnosed and misunderstood.

They are humans and should be treated with dignity and respect.

A person has to be willing to accept the fact that he or she has a mental illness before the healing process can begin. God can not cure a person with mental illness it depends on a person's level of faith.

Mental illness can be controlled if the person gets assistance for their disorder, overall with God involved all things are possible.

They need help like anyone else. So pray and help them.

I personally believe that mental illness is a generational curse.

They're human beings as well as normal human beings.

God made them also; and they are people that need assistance at times. All people need help before they die.

Each community should have persons capable of helping those with mental illness. I believe there is so much mental illness because of stress and environmental conditions.

They need someone try to help them with reaching their capabilities.

They need to be loved. You should have patience with them. We all have some type of illness and we have to handle the issue. I believe that they can make it with help.

We as a community need to get more involved with the mentally ill.

They still are human beings and there is still hope.

They need extra love and caring for.

We have an obligation to win the confidence of people and then and only then can we direct them to the appropriate agencies / programs that they will receive help from.

They are people too and we need to remember that.

One person said "Pray church pray".

God can cure anything.

You shouldn't judge them or look down on them. If you have time get to know them or help them because the same can happen to someone in your family. You would not want anyone to mistreat your family members or friends.

If you are not trained to deal with them I feel you should leave it for the proper authorities.

You need to have patience with them. Listen to what they are saying. Always be calm, never overly verbal with them, and let them know you care and that you want to help them.

They need someone to care. They also need to be loved. They are very hard to understand but they are people too. God can do all things.

They need to stay on their medicine and pray to God for help. Someone needs to counsel them, possibly a mental professional and a Christian professional. Can a person that is mentally ill be also mentally retarded, I don't know that will depend; but I say yes, it is mental retardation but I have questions.

My comment is that anybody can be healed if it's in God's will. But, if you know someone with a mental illness and you know that they are not getting any help, try to steer them in the right direction to get help, even if you have to take them.

We should show them respect / concerns just like normal people. Remember that God is love and we should show love.

The government has cut the money to help the mentally ill. We citizens should contact those in government to help the mentally ill.

Mentally ill persons are God's precious love ones no less than anyone else. Together with all persons they have value and offer something to the community of faith.

It (Mental illness) occurs in families of course it can just come on a person as they age.

Pray for the person and seek ways to help in any way.

We should do more to educate people on the signs of mental illness. Also be aware of services for those that are mentally ill.

Above were the various comments of people even though some of them were incorrect for dealing with those that are mentally ill.

SURVEY RESULTS OF THE 25 THAT WERE INTERVIEWED

Age of Person completing survey 24 – 78

Male 14   Female 11

Christian 24   Non-Christian 1

1. Can you become mentally ill because you spend long periods of time with someone that has a mental illness?

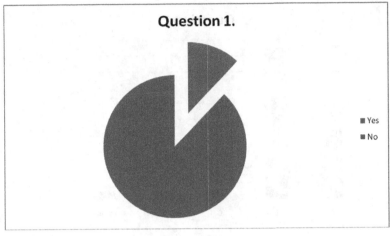

Yes 3   No 22

Answer:

There was very little concern with becoming mentally ill by being around someone that is mentally ill for long periods of time.

2. Who should deal with the people that are on the streets and in the community that have mental illness?

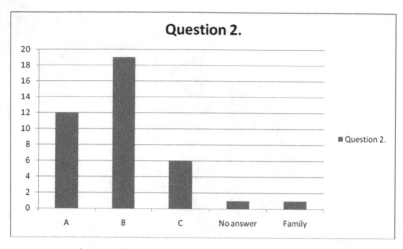

a. the police b. providers only c. you d. They should be by themselves

a. 12   b. 19   c. 6   No answer 1   Family 1

Answer:

The provider company and police were the favorite choices that should deal with people that are mentally ill in the community.

3. Do you have an obligation to help the mentally ill?

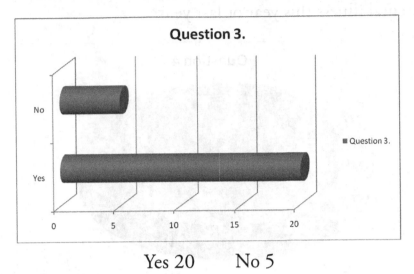

Yes 20   No 5

Answer:

This question sparked an overwhelming choice of yes and sparked questions of what could be done for someone and the need for people getting the proper training to be able to assist people that are mentally ill.

4. Have you assisted in any positive way someone that has mental illness this year or last year?

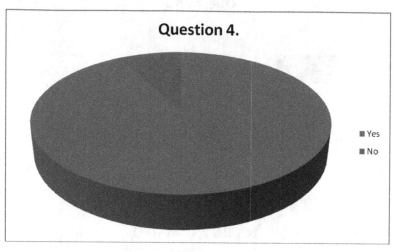

Yes 23 No 2

Answer:

The response about helping someone in the last year with mental illness was a majority yes.

5. Have you lived with someone that has a mental illness? If yes, how long?

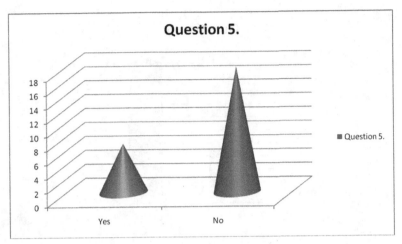

Yes 7   No 18   How Long from 2yrs – 40yrs

Answer:

The number was greater for the answer no than the answer yes concerning those that have lived with someone that has mental illness.

6. What can you do to help someone get assistance with their condition of mental illness?

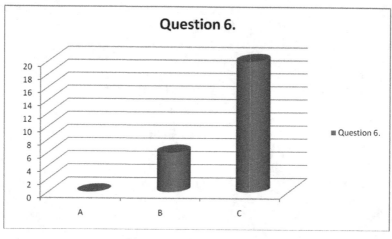

a. let them along   b. call the police   c. get to know them

a. 0   b. 6   c. 19

Answer:

Truly getting to know people that are different is important for the individual with a mental illness and also important for those that are supposedly normal to increase the opportunity to help someone that needs help.

7. Should the Christian church do something to help people with mental illness?

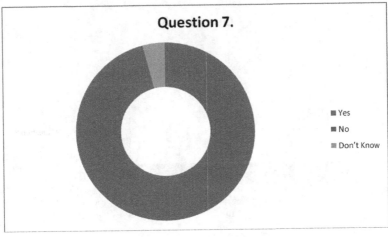

Yes 24   No 0   Don't know 1

Answer:

There seems to be a strong belief that the Christian church should do something to help people that are mentally ill even though no one could tell what should be done by the church other than pray.

8. Do some individuals inherit mental illnesses from their parents or other ancestors in their family?

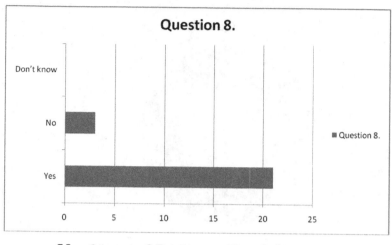

Yes 21   No 3   Don't know 1

Answer:

Some mentally ill people do inherit their mental illness from an ancestor but not all mental illness is inherited. Some mental illnesses are biological and some chemically induced.

9. Is mental illness and mental retardation the same thing?

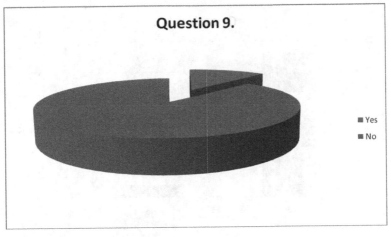

Yes 3   No 22

Answer:

Mental Illness is not the same as mentally retardation but a person can be mentally retarded and mentally ill also.

10. Can God cure a person from mental illness?

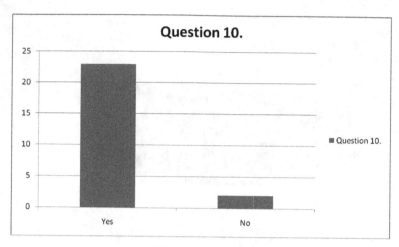

Yes 23 No 2

Answer:

God can heal who he wants to heal and if he doesn't heal someone it is because he does not want to heal them.

Final Question of the 25 people that were surveyed:
What other comments do you have about people with mental illness?

These are the various comments that people made concerning people with mental illness:

Mental illness is a serious medical condition. Anyone and everyone should get involved and do what it takes in all efforts of getting some help.

I'm hopeful and prayerful that God will continue to provide help for them.

I believe that the police, community, family and church should all help people who cannot help themselves. We can't help everybody but if we help one person we have done a lot and God is pleased.

Anyone can get mental illness at any time if you do not have an outlet for the pressure that you can experience.

The church needs to pray for people that are mentally ill.

The family of the person that is mentally ill should deal with the person on the streets and in the community.

I have assisted my best friend that is mentally ill.

We must help find the mentally ill person help through an agency and get them on medication.

You need to get to know the mentally ill person and assist them by helping them get to the resources that will help him.

Community and family members need to get more involved.

Above were the various comments of people even though some of them were incorrect for dealing with those that are mentally ill.

What can be done now to improve the relationship of the Christian church and those that are mentally ill?

This is a question that can possibly be asked and answered in many different ways for years to come. There are multiplicities of answers to this question even in this present day, but the one that I am giving is the one according to my research, my thoughts and my beliefs of the way to improve the relationships of these important sectors of society. There is a need to better understand what to do or what to say to people that are different because of mental deficits that they are experiencing that makes them a little or a lot more different from others. Training should be done not just for the minister or clergy. Training should also be available for the lay people and anyone else that wants to help someone that is mentally ill and needs assistance from someone.

The church should feel more obligated and get more involved in helping people that are on the streets and in need of mental health assistance. I think it takes more than feeding or giving can goods to the homeless once or twice a year that are dealing with mental illness. It's going to take an involved Christian community of people that are concerned about the life of someone besides themselves to help effectuate change in the lives of many. The question is how do you energize people to get involved with people when it seems as if most people are caught up in their own issues and not thinking about the lives and issues of others. What are the resources that are available to get people more aware of the needs of the mentally ill and challenging them to just help someone?

I think the churches should and can do much more and get more involved with helping people get the help they need that have mental illness. I feel that the church needs to get more involved with individuals and their problems outside the doors of the church as well as people inside the church. Inside the church there is comfort and also a since of safety that causes us to want to stay inside our comfort zone. What occurs inside the church today that is called ministry makes us feel what occurs in the church is the only thing that is important in ministry and we disregard those that are in need outside the doors of the church.

I believe there is a need for mission work in our communities with those that are mentally ill and out on the streets without any possibility of hope for their future. Missions includes more than providing food and clothes for those in need, the need simply goes beyond that. There seems to be a need for missions directed towards giving assistance to those that cannot function in the community or can't function well enough to maintain a lifestyle that is beyond the Melancholy and disheveled lifestyle that most people with mental illness live with.

They are without hope, confused and on the streets in our community and it seem as if no one is willing to truly get them the help that they need.

There is need for more training for the pastors and minsters of the various churches, teaching the clergy what to do to get assistance for those that are hurting mentally in their community. Now this does not mean that ministers do not care or are not involved in their community. Ministers generally know who is hurting in their community but this does not mean that quite a few are not equipped with knowledge and training that is needed to make a difference. There is information and resources that ministers need to be able to help those that are really hurting and in need of someone that they can talk to and help empower them to get off the streets. Some use drugs and don't want to get off drugs because of self-medicating themselves to get through their mental health problems or mental disorders. I have had individuals to tell me that they drink or do drugs because it helps them to cope with their problems even if it is only for a limited time that they are high. Some people have said they do drugs because they are hearing voices in their head or seeing visions because of military combat or other traumatic events in their life. Additionally, they said using drugs and / or staying drunk for long periods of time helps them get beyond their present situation or issues that are so hard for them to deal with any other way. It sounds like it might be untrue but until we walk in someone else's shoes it is hard to understand.

There was a question from an individual that completed one of surveys, it was should help come from the pastor or ministers in the community? Well I think this will be debated by the pastors, ministers, church members and others in the community for a long time to come, because everyone has different opinions as to what help should be given. I think with the proper training such as crisis intervention training for pastors or ministers by mental health entities. Proper training will assist the pastors and minsters and will give them the confidence that they will get more involved and feel less apprehensive about helping those that are mentally ill.

At this point I do not know if there will be any change in the Christian community as to the involvement or lack of involvement in the life of the mentally ill. I feel the Lord will have to intervene so that change will occur in the way that the Christian community reacts to the mentally ill.

There is some concern about the lack of assistance from most churches in the various communities that will truly effectuate change spiritually. A lot of churches are not dealing with the problem of mental illness on the streets and in the community for whatever reason. The reason could be fear of the mentally ill or lack of training in this area.

This is a key example from Tom Skinner about the lack of churches in the community making a difference with people that is in need.

> "One of the things that keeps the church from being a voice in the community is that the Church doesn't do the things of God in locations where the world will be able to see it. Most Christians reserve all of their teaching and preaching and testifying for one another.

> The problem is that Christians tend to shy away from people of the world because they fear they might lose their testimonies. There are many creative ways for the people of God to make an impact on communities. All they need to do is pull off restrictive shackles. The Word of God says not to be of the world, but to be in it.

> Jesus said Christians should be lights. The function of a light is to scatter darkness, however, what God's people have been doing is taking out a flashlight at noon and singing, (this little light of mine, I'm gonna let it shine). Light is not needed in the sun. Light is needed where it is darkness. That's where God's people have to be a voice. That's where we have to exert influence. We must go to the darkest places and turn the light on." (Birchett, 1992 p. 165, 166)

Mental Illness is a type of darkness and it's a challenge to deal with the person that is mentally ill by the individuals that are not aware of how to interact with them. Mental illness is also a darkness because those that need to help cannot see the answer for their situation.

People are worried about dealing with people that have mental illness because of fear of being attack by them or spit on by them because of hearing about how aggressive they can be. But what is missed most of the time is that mentally ill people are just like us they want respect and they want help for their need.

They try to hear what is being said to them even though it can be difficult because of their problem. They want to be connected to the rest of the world but the rest of us at times do not want to be connected to them. They do not know how to tell someone about their situation or confused condition in which they need help. People that are mentally ill are operating in dysfunction and it is their dysfunction that has become normal for them because the dysfunction is what they know and it has become their normal way of living. In some cases, the dysfunction is where they want to stay because it has become the norm for them and they have begun to believe that there is no other option for them because of their condition. Other questions are, is there any help for someone that is mentally ill, is there help from anyone that cares and want to make a difference? Is there any help that can come from the Christian community or from the churches? Help can only begin from within us in the form of desire to help someone along the way and then our talking and living will not be in vain. God challenges all of us to be about his work and to be our brothers and sisters' keeper. The Lord keeps us in midst of our troubles, struggles and mishaps of life and surely we can look after our fellow man that is in need of us assisting them in their time of need and misdirection.

"What is the church's responsibility to the mentally ill? I have concluded that Mental Illness, despite the potential baggage of the worldview of psychology, is inherently a truthful enough category to be useful in describing a phenomenon in the real world. While there are very controversial and ongoing conversations regarding the Biblical analysis of mental illness and the interpretation of Biblical passages about mental illness, we cannot reasonably deny that mental illness, as a human experience understood today in the language of medical diagnosis, did exist in the Bible and is all around us today.

The mentally and emotionally ill are part of every church. They make up part of the body of Christ. They are persons baptized, professing faith, participating in fellowship, worship and ministry. They are ministers, teachers and pastors. They are the fathers, mothers, young adults, college students and singles in our churches. At times they are our children. Certainly they are part of the community every church seeks to reach.

Churches that choose to ignore mental illness are making the decision to deny a valid part of the human story." (Spencer, 2005, Internet)

So apparently the mentally ill are not just in the streets they are in the church and in our homes. They are closer to us than we realize or wants to realize. Whether we realize it or not the mentally ill are not just in our communities but right in front of our face at times and we all have an obligation to assist each other.

The mission of the church is first of all to save those that are lost and the mission also seems to be to feed the world's hungry. But there is a need for some mission work in the life of those that are mentally ill and are suffering from the disconnection from anyone showing love for them. The Apostle Paul went on various missionary journeys but he had to be prepared for the mission by the Lord himself. But when Paul became equipped for the mission and afterward he had sought out others that were familiar with the work that was needed to be done, Paul then went to work preaching the gospel of Jesus Christ effectuating a change the lives of thousands of people. Mission work for the lost is still needed, but there is also mission work needed for the mentally ill and those that are distraught and separated from the world because of being distraught and confused. We all need to do our part or do something to improve the life of the disconnected mentally ill person.

"Serious Mental Illness and faith: what to do?

Had a meeting today with two people from UPENN (one a prof) who are working to break down barriers for those with Serious Mental Illness (SMI). They have found that folks with SMI are quite likely to acknowledge spiritual or religious beliefs and identity. And yet, these folks say there are two serious roadblocks for finding support. First, the church does not seem particularly open to folks with SMI. Second, mental health professionals are either unsupportive or downright negative about the faith/beliefs of those with SMI.

Actually, the UPENN folks said they had more hope that the church would be open to developing policies and systems for supporting the mentally ill than they had hope in influencing the mental health professionals that pay attention to one's faith is an essential part of their healing and rehabilitation.

One of the church's challenges is that they need to develop strategies for the long haul. If the church is going to do well with someone with bipolar or schizophrenia, then they need to realize how best to pace the response. I think some churches are willing to throw lots of resources at the person in an effort to try to solve the problem. And if the person is not progressing as they had hoped, then the interest in helping dies off. Hence you have folks with SMI making serial connections with the churches in their area." (Phil Monroe, 2007)

Now that is interesting to see that we can move to quickly too help someone without giving opportunity to set up rapport and learning more about the individual as a person with a condition versus dealing with the condition and not learning the person. So to help the person with the mental illness we need to get to know them and their uniqueness as a person along with getting to know about their mental disorder. This is truly the first step in the process to effectuate a change in the life of the individual with mental illness. Then we will be able to possibly give the appropriate directions and the needed resources that will bring about a change in their lives. Christian love for others and the proper training is what will help us to work together to get our mentally ill brothers and sisters the help that they need. Paul says in 1 Corinthians Chapter 13 verse 1-3, Though I speak with the tongues of men and of angels, and have not charity (love), I am become a sounding brass, or a tinkling cymbal. And though I have the gift of prophecy, and understand all mysteries, and all knowledge; and though I have all faith, so that I could remove mountains, and have not charity (love), I am nothing. And though I bestow all my goods to feed the poor, and though I give my body to be burned, and have not charity (love), it profited me nothing. Love is what can get us through arguments, controversies and misunderstanding and love can bring us to the point of helping our brothers and sisters that are in our churches, in our communities and out there on skid row with mental health and drug issues.

These are some of the mental illnesses that usually exist in those that have need and are living on the streets with mental health issues:

Schizophrenia Disorders, Bipolar Disorders, Major Depression Disorders, Anxiety Disorders, Posttraumatic Stress Disorder, Substance Abuse and Addictive Disorders, Dual mental Health and Substance Abuse Disorders, Alzheimer Disease and/or Vascular Disease, Traumatic Brain Injury(TBI) and Personality Disorders to name a few. These constitutes a need for help from every angle of our society including the Christian community.

DEFINITION OF TERMS

Acquiesce - To agree or express agreement.

Agilely - In a nimble or agile manner; with quickness and lightness and ease.

Biochemical - Of or relating to biochemistry; involving chemical processes in living organisms

Bipolar - Of or relating to manic depressive illness.

Enrichment - Act of making fuller or more meaningful or rewarding.

Epistemologies - The philosophical theory of knowledge.

Explicitly - In an explicit manner. Precisely and clearly communicated or readily observable; leaving nothing to implication

Illness - Impairment of normal physiological function affecting part or all of an organism.

Hara-kiri - Ritual suicide by self-disembowelment on a sword; practiced by samurai in the traditional Japanese society.

Hypothesis - A proposal intended to explain certain facts or observations.

Maladaptive - Showing faulty adaptation.

Multiplicities - The property of being multiple. It's a large number.

Mental - Involving the mind or an intellectual process

Methodology - The branch of philosophy that analyzes the principles and procedures of inquiry in a particular discipline.

Nomothetic - (psychology) relating to or involving the search for abstract universal principles.

Pejorative - Expressing disapproval.

Polarisation - The condition of having or giving polarity.

Schizophrenia - Any of several psychotic disorders characterized by distortions of reality and disturbances of thought and language and withdrawal from social contact.

Tangentially - In passing. Pertaining to or of the nature of a tangent; being or moving in the direction of a tangent. Merely touching; slightly connected: tangential information.

Theoretical - Concerned primarily with theories or hypotheses rather than practical considerations.

Variables - Something that is likely to vary; something that is subject to variation.

REFERENCES

Birchett, C. (1992). *Biblical strategies for a community in crisis what african americans can do.* Chicago, Illinois: Urban Ministries, Inc.

Cook, C. (2009). *Spirituality and psychiatry.* (p. 256, 257). Glasgow, Uk. : The Royal College of Psychiatrists, Bell & Bain Limited.

Corrigan, P. W. (2005). *On the stigma of mental illness practical strategies for research and social change.* (p. 284). Washington, D.C: American Psychological Association

Eshun, S. & Gurung, (Eds.) R. A. R. (2009). *Cultural and Mental Health Sociocultural Influences, Theory and Practice* (p. p.7, 116). The Atrium, Southern Gate, Chichester, West Sussex, PO 19 8SQ, United Kingdom: Wiley- Blackwell John Wiley & Sons Ltd.

Gregory (Ed.), R. L. (2004). *The Oxford Companion to the Mind Second Edition.* (p. 576) New York: Oxford University Press Inc.

Koenig, H. G. (2005). *Faith & mental health religious resources for healing.* (p. 260, 261). Conshohocken, Pa. : Templeton Foundation Press

Koenig, H. G. (2005). *Faith & mental health religious resources for healing.* . (p. 178, 179). West Conshohocken, Pa. : Templeton Foundation Press

Lefley, H. P. & Pedersen, (Eds.) P. B. (1986). *Cross-Cultural Training for Mental Health Professionals* (p. p. 131, 132). 2600 South First Street Springfield, Illinois 62708. : Charles C. Thomas Publisher

McNamara, P. (Ed.) (2006). *Where God and Science Meet how Brain and Evolutionary Studies Alter Our Understanding of Religion Volume 3 The Psychology of Religious Experience* (Vol. 3, p. Page 37). 88 Post Road West, Westport, CT 06881: Greenwood Publishing Group, Inc., Praeger Publishers.

Monroe, Phil P. (2007, June 26). *Musings of a Christian psychologist - serious mental illness and faith: what to do?*

Nelson (Ed.) T. D. (2009). *Handbook of Prejudice, Stereotyping, and Discrimination* (p. p.9). 270 Madison Avenue New York, NY 10016: Psychology Press, Taylor & Frances Group

Snowden, L. R. (October 2012). Health and mental health policies' role in better understanding and closing African - white American disparities in treatment access and quality of care. *American Psychologist*

Journal of the American Psychologist Association, 67(7), p.526. doi: ISSN 0003-066X

Spencer, M. (2005, November 28). Internet monk- The Christian and the mental illness v: The church and the mentally ill.

Tausig, M. (2007). The Blackwell encyclopedia of sociology. In G. Ritzer (Ed.), Oxford OX4 2DQ, UK. : Blackwell Publishing

King James Bibles

APPENDIXES

a. Timetable for the research:
    1) Timetable for survey research – This part of the research took approximately 3 months.

    2) Timetable for total research of paper – Total research approximately 8 months

b. Data and collection of information
    1) The data was collected to deal with the hypothesis of there being a disconnection between the church and the community.

Printed in the United States
By Bookmasters